THE MAN WHO INVENTED TELEVISION

The Genius of Philo T. Farnsworth

Titles in the *Genius Inventors and Their Great Ideas* Series:

...RS AND THEIR GREAT IDEAS

THE MAN WHO INVENTED TELEVISION

The Genius of Philo T. Farnsworth

Edwin Brit Wyckoff

Enslow Elementary

an imprint of

 Enslow Publishers, Inc.

40 Industrial Road
Box 398
Berkeley Heights, NJ 07922
USA

http://www.enslow.com

Content Advisors
Kent M. Farnsworth
Son of Philo T. Farnsworth
Steward, Farnsworth Archives:
  http://www.philotfarnsworth.com

Evan I. Schwartz
Author, *The Last Lone Inventor: A Tale of Genius, Deceit &*
  the Birth of Television

Series Literacy Consultant
Allan A. De Fina, Ph.D.
Past President of the New Jersey Reading Association
Chairperson, Derpartment of Literacy Education
New Jersey City University

Acknowledgment
The publisher thanks Kent M. Farnsworth for providing many insights
and photos for the publication of this book.

Enslow Elementary, an imprint of Enslow Publishers, Inc.
Enslow Elementary® is a registered trademark of Enslow Publishers, Inc.

Original edition published as *The Teen Who Invented Television: Philo T. Farnsworth and His Awesome Invention*, in 2008.

Library of Congress Cataloging-in-Publication Data

Wyckoff, Edwin Brit.
  The man who invented television : the genius of Philo T. Farnsworth / Edwin Brit Wyckoff.
      p. cm. — (Genius inventors and their great ideas)
  Includes index.
  Summary: "Read about Philo T. Farnsworth and how he invented the television"— Provided by publisher.
      ISBN 978-0-7660-4139-4
  1. Farnsworth, Philo Taylor, 1906-1971—Juvenile literature. 2. Electrical engineers—United States—Biography—Juvenile literature. 3. Television—History—Juvenile literature. I. Title.
  TK6635.F3W92 2013
  621.3880092—dc23
  [B]
                                    2012013973

Future editions:
Paperback ISBN: 978-1-4644-0209-8   EPUB ISBN: 978-1-4645-1122-6
Single-User PDF ISBN: 978-1-4646-1122-3   Multi-User PDF ISBN: 978-0-7660-5751-7

Printed in the United States of America
042013 Lake Book Manufacturing, Inc., Melrose Park, IL
10 9 8 7 6 5 4 3 2 1

To Our Readers: We have done our best to make sure all Internet addresses in this book were active and appropriate when we went to press. However, the author and the publisher have no control over and assume no liability for the material available on those Internet sites or on other Web sites they may link to. Any comments or suggestions can be sent by e-mail to comments@enslow.com or to the address on the back cover.

♻ Enslow Publishers, Inc., is committed to printing our books on recycled paper. The paper in every book contains 10% to 30% post-consumer waste (PCW). The cover board on the outside of each book contains 100% PCW. Our goal is to do our part to help young people and the environment too!

Photo Credits: Alvis E. Hendley, p. 25; Courtesy MagazineArt.org, p. 11; Courtesy Steve McVoy, Early Television Foundation, p. 14; Farnsworth Archives, pp. 5 (top) 6, 8, 9, 18, 19, 21, 26, 28, 29, 34, 36, 37; Library of Congress, p. 33; Manuscripts Division, University of Utah Libraries, pp. 20, 23, 32, 38 (portrait); NASA/Scan by Kipp Teague, p. 38 (background); Schomburg Center for Research in Black Culture/ Photographs and Prints Division/New York Pulbic Library, p. 13; Utah State Historical Society, all rights reserved., pp. 1, 3, 5, (bottom). Wisconsin Historical Society, p.16.

Cover Photo: AP Images: Philo T. Farnsworth; Shutterstock: Television

CONTENTS

Philo T. Farnsworth, 1936

Chapter 1

Dangerous Dreams

Three powerful horses were plowing the potato fields back and forth, slowly and steadily. Fourteen-year-old Philo Farnsworth held the reins loosely. He seemed to be slipping into sleep as some of the reins fell from his hands. His father could see a terrible accident about to happen. Shouting would have scared the horses. So without a word, he raced across the field and scooped up the fallen reins. The horses stopped. Philo snapped wide awake. His father was very angry. But Philo's eyes were filled with excitement.

He had just dreamed up how to build a magnetic lock for an automobile. That idea won him twenty-five dollars in a contest run by *Science and Invention*

This is Philo's father, Lewis Farnsworth. The two of them were very close.

magazine. Twenty-five dollars was a lot of money in those days, when an ice-cream cone cost only a nickel.

Philo Taylor Farnsworth had been born on August 19, 1906, in Beaver, Utah. He had two younger brothers and two sisters. His parents, Lewis and Serena, were farmers. They were always looking for cheaper, better land on which to raise their crops. In 1918, when Philo was about twelve, the family packed up and moved from Utah to Rigby, Idaho. Young Philo drove the horses that pulled one of their covered wagons. He was dreaming about inventions all the way.

The new farm was wonderful. Unlike most farms in that time, it had electric lights. The children found a pile of old, broken motors to play with. For Philo, the biggest treasure was up in the attic. There he found lots of science magazines with names like *Modern Electrics, Electrical Experimenter,* and *Radio News.* He read them over and over.

Philo was born in this cabin in Beaver, Utah. At the time the town was called Indian Creek.

He learned how airplanes lifted off the ground and how radios were built. He read about ideas for the future, like spaceships and collecting energy from the sun. He thought he could someday invent things, too—but first he had to learn everything he could about science.

One day, the lights went out on the farm. The electric generator had stopped working. Repairmen were called to fix it. After they were gone, the lights went out again. Philo thought he had seen the men make a mistake. The whole family watched as Philo fixed the mistake in minutes. The lights blazed on again.

Philo liked to read these magazines. They told of ideas about life in the future.

Chapter 2

Flying Pictures

Radios were new in the early 1900s. People would sit and watch them, even though radios just played music and told news. There was really nothing to see.

Philo's scientific magazines began reporting about something called television. They said it would make pictures "fly" through the air on radio. But television was an idea that still had to be figured out.

Philo was captivated. He dreamed that he would make a fortune by bringing pictures into every home. He was sure that the television systems described in his magazines would not work very well. He knew that he could do better.

People like to sit around listening to the radio together.

Philo's magazines described television systems that were mechanical. This television receiver, made by John Logie Baird, used a spinning wheel inside.

Philo did not want to use moving parts like spinning wheels. They were not fast enough to make a clear picture. He believed in using electrons. Electrons are tiny parts of every atom. Water, rocks, air, people—every piece of matter is made of atoms with electrons. Philo wanted to learn how to use them to make electronic television pictures.

It was the summer of 1921, and Philo was just fifteen years old. He searched for one big idea that would allow him to use electrons. Hour after hour, he held the leather reins as the farm horses slowly worked the fields. Squinting in the sun, he would watch row after row of earth and crops line up. All of a sudden he saw something exciting. He imagined row after row of electrons lining up to make pictures. As the electrons moved, the pictures moved, almost like crops blowing in the wind.

In his mind's eye, he saw a camera shaped like a glass bottle. Light from a picture that traveled through the flat end of the bottle would be changed into rows of

Philo was riding a disk harrow like this one when he had his idea. When the disks were dragged through the dirt, many even rows were created. This way a farmer could quickly prepare a field for planting seeds.

electrons inside. Another bottle could be the television screen. Rows of electrons inside the bottle would become a picture flashed onto the flat end. Philo could almost shout with happiness. He was going to invent television.

Chapter 3

The Amazing Student

In September, Philo entered Rigby High School. First-year science classes were too easy for him. He wanted to skip to senior science classes. The teacher, Justin Tolman, first said no. Philo asked him every day. Finally, Mr. Tolman let him sit in the back of the room during the class.

After school one day, Mr. Tolman found Philo filling every inch of the blackboard with drawings. Philo started talking faster and faster—about television. He took a page from his teacher's notebook to make more drawings. Someday that page of scribbles would be very, very important. Mr. Tolman told Philo to keep quiet about television or someone could steal his ideas.

HIGH SCHOOL, RIGBY, IDAHO.

Rigby High School in Rigby, Idaho, was where Philo became friends with his science teacher, Justin Tolman.

Although he was busy with thinking, Philo still found time for fun. He learned how to play the violin and joined a band. This serious young man was a great dancer, a good actor, and would become a very good tennis player.

In the cold, hard winter of 1924, Philo's father returned from a long trip and became very sick. He died

Philo's Television

This is the sketch of a television camera that Philo drew for Mr. Tolman. Light from a picture hits the camera on the left, labeled "optical image." Electrons scan the optical image and change it into an electronic signal on the right, labeled "electron image."

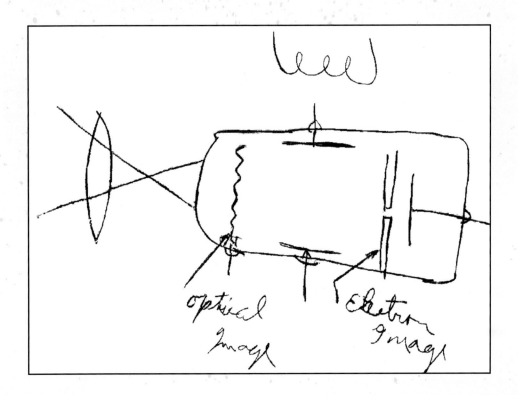

Philo (center) acted in the play *Charm School* at Brigham Young University.

Young Philo

when Philo was only seventeen. The boy had to work to support the family. He earned a high school diploma and had a real love for learning but no way to pay for college.

Still, Philo enrolled at Brigham Young University in Provo, Utah. He worked as a school janitor to pay for his university classes. He still loved music and dancing and

Elma "Pem" Gardner

parties. He also started dating Elma Gardner, his neighbor. Everyone called her Pem. Philo was so quiet that Pem was not sure he cared about her.

Philo took the test to become a Navy officer. His score was second highest in the whole country. He was accepted by the United States Naval Academy in Annapolis, Maryland. But once he was there, he realized that the government would own inventions he thought up while he was in the Navy. His mother told the school she needed him at home, and he was allowed to leave the school.

Les Gorrell (left), Philo (center), and George Everson worked together to start creating electronic television.

Chapter 4

Meeting the Money Men

Philo went back to college for another year, but money problems forced him to drop out. He took a full-time job working for two smart young men. George Everson and Leslie Gorrell were in the business of raising money for charities that helped needy people in Salt Lake City. Working late one night, he started telling them his ideas. He talked faster and faster—about television.

Everson suddenly asked, "How much? How much to make a working model?" That was a scary question. Philo answered, "Five thousand dollars." Everson offered, "We'll invest six thousand. And the workshop has to be in California."

Philo was only nineteen, and he was starting a new life. He telephoned Pem. "Can you be ready to get married in three days?" So Philo and Pem married on May 27, 1926. They took a train to Los Angeles, California, just one day after their wedding.

In this laboratory at 202 Green Street, San Francisco, Philo built the first electronic television system.

Cliff Gardner, Pem's brother, found a new way to make the glass "bottles" Philo needed for his television system.

Their apartment was very small. The dining room table was covered with Philo's inventions. Closets were jammed with his equipment. Pem learned how to spot weld metal together and how to make technical drawings. George Everson took charge of cooking. All of them would eat and work together six nights a week.

Their $6,000 ran out quickly. Everson and Gorrell went looking for investors. They found a rich banker, James Fagan. He growled, "This television is a … fool idea. But somebody ought to put money into it." He gave them $25,000.

The team moved to San Francisco, California. Philo bought new tools and hired Cliff Gardner, Pem's brother. Cliff quickly learned how to blow fiery hot glass into tubes with a special flat end. Some of the tubes became the camera, which Philo called an image dissector. Others were turned into receivers, which would show the pictures made by lines of electrons. The image dissector and the receiver were the "bottles" that Philo had seen in his mind in 1921 on his family's farm.

It was time to tell the whole world Philo's secret ideas. On January 7, 1927, Philo asked the government for patents to protect his camera and receiver. He tested his system in his laboratory in San Francisco in September of that year. He turned on the power. He flipped all the

Philo holds an image dissector. In front of him is an early television camera.

This early television picture of Pem from 1930 shows the lines of the electrons.

switches. Everyone waited and worried. Slowly, an image of a line formed on the receiver. "There you are," Philo said, "electronic television."

In 1928, a newspaper in San Francisco ran an article about Philo, with a huge headline:

MAN'S INVENTION TO REVOLUTIONIZE TELEVISION. FARNSWORTH'S SYSTEM EMPLOYS NO MOVING PARTS.

In August 1930, Philo was given two patents for his television camera and receiver. He was only twenty-four years old.

Chapter 5

The Patent War

A very important businessman visited Philo's laborabory to see the system work. David Sarnoff was the president of the giant Radio Corporation of America, or RCA. He looked at everything very carefully. He said, "There is nothing we need here." Then he shocked everybody. Sarnoff offered to buy the whole laboratory for $100,000. Philo would have to go to work for RCA. His answer was a flat, final, no.

Sarnoff did not like being told no by anybody. But he wanted Philo's inventions. He would fight to get them. His company had lots of lawyers. They attacked Philo in court, saying that he did not really invent electronic television.

screen

This is a Farnsworth Television Receiver from 1930.

David Sarnoff knew that Philo's television patents were worth millions of dollars.

Philo had to prove that he had told someone his television ideas in 1922 when he was just a teenager. He thought and thought. Then he came up with just two words—Justin Tolman.

Philo's lawyers went looking for his old science teacher. Mr. Tolman went down to his basement. When he climbed back up the stairs, he was waving a page from his old notebook. It was covered with Philo's drawing from way back in 1922.

Tough, powerful David Sarnoff and his lawyers lost the court case in 1935. Philo was exhausted.

The United States Patent Office approved each of Philo's ideas and drawings with a numbered patent.

A patent grant says powerful things:

- The ideas are workable.

- The ideas are new—no one else has yet presented them.

- If people want to use the ideas, they have to pay the owner of the patent money, called a royalty.

Justin Tolman, here with Philo, helped him to win
the court case against David Sarnoff and RCA.

Sarnoff may have lost the fight, but he was a good businessman. In October 1939, he offered to pay one million dollars over ten years to use Philo's patents and pay a royalty every time he used the invention. Sarnoff hated paying royalties. But he had to pay Philo.

The farm boy who invented electronic television when he was only fifteen years old never stopped dreaming and inventing. He received more than one hundred patents for new and better radios, television systems, and military tools. On July 20, 1969, he watched American astronauts walking on the moon. The astronauts sent back sharp, clear pictures. The pictures traveled 238,900 miles from the moon using a very small version of Philo's image dissector.

Philo's inventions created new industries. They have made it possible for doctors to send tiny television cameras inside a human body. And they let hundreds of millions of people watch events on television as they happen.

Screen

Philo adjusts the dials as he looks into an early television receiver.
The round object at the top right is the speaker.

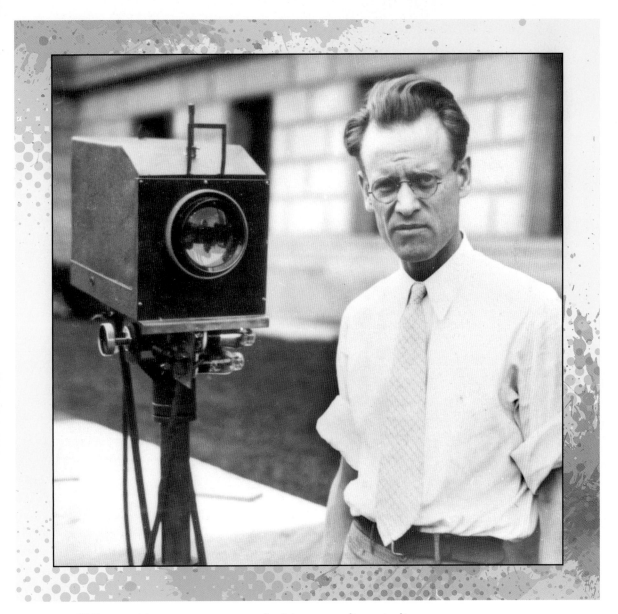

Philo would go on to own a television recording studio.
Here he stands with the first mobile television camera.

Once Philo saw astronauts walking on the moon on television, he knew his invention had been worth all the work.

Philo T. Farnsworth died in Salt Lake City on March 11, 1971. He was sixty-four years old. In 1984, he was elected to the National Inventors Hall of Fame. The young farm boy from Utah had spent his whole life studying, thinking, and dreaming science. Through his love for new ideas and inventions, Philo Farnsworth had invented himself.

TIMELINE

1906—Born on August 19 in Beaver, Utah.

1922—Shows television drawings to his science teacher, Justin Tolman.

1924—Father dies; Philo attends Brigham Young University for two years.

1926—Creates partnership with George Everson and Leslie Gorrell to develop television; marries Elma "Pem" Gardner and moves to California.

1927—Files patents for television system; tests system successfully in San Francisco.

1930—Is granted patents for television camera and receiver.

1935—Radio Corporation of America loses court case against Philo.

1939—RCA pays one million dollars to license Philo's television patents.

1971— Dies on March 11 in Salt Lake City, Utah; buried in Provo, Utah.

1984—Is elected to National Inventors Hall of Fame by United States Patent Office.

YOU BE THE INVENTOR!

So you want to be an inventor? You can do it! First, you need a terrific idea.

Got a problem? No problem!

Many inventions begin when someone thinks of a great solution to a problem. One cold day in 1994, 10-year-old K.K. Gregory was building a snow fort. Soon, she had snow between her mittens and her coat sleeve. Her wrists were cold and wet. She found some scraps of fabric around the house, and used them to make a tube that would fit around her wrist. She cut a thumbhole in the tube to make a kind of fingerless glove, and called it a "Wristie." Wearing mittens over her new invention, her wrists stayed nice and warm when she played outside. Today, the Wristie business is booming.

Now it's your turn. Maybe, like K.K. Gregory, you have an idea for something new that would make your life better or easier. Perhaps you can think of a way improve an everyday item. Twelve year-old Becky Schroeder became the youngest female ever to receive a U.S. patent after she invented a glow-in-the dark clipboard that allowed people to write in the dark. Do you like to play sports or board games? James Naismith, inspired by a game he used to play as a boy, invented a new game he called basketball.

Let your imagination run wild. You never know where it will take you.

Research it!

You have a great idea! Now What?

First, you'll want to make sure that nobody else has thought of your idea. You wouldn't want to spend hours developing your new invention, only to find that someone else beat you to it. Google Patents can help you find out whether your idea is original.

Bring it to life!

If no one else has thought of your idea, congratulations! Write it down in a logbook or journal. Write the date and your initials for every entry you make. If you file a patent for your invention later, this will help you prove that you were the first person to think of it. The most important thing about this logbook is that pages cannot be added or subtracted. You can buy a bound notebook at any office supply store.

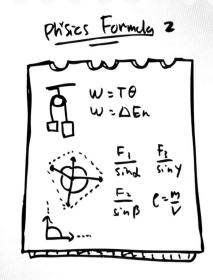

Draw several different pictures of your invention in your logbook. Try sketching views from above, below, and to the side. Show how big each part of your invention should be.

Build a model. Don't be discouraged if it doesn't work at first. You may have to experiment with different designs and materials. That's part of the fun! Take pictures of everything, and tape them into your logbook.

Try out your invention on your friends and family. If they have any suggestions to make it better, you may want to build another model. Perfect your invention, and give it a clever name.

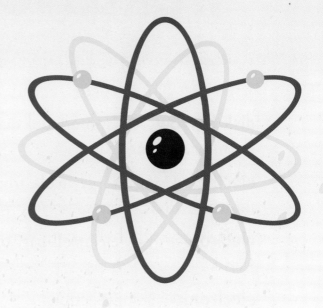

Patent it!

Do you want to sell your invention? You'll want to apply for a patent. Holding a patent to your invention means that no one else can make, use, or sell your invention in the U.S. without your permission. It prevents others from making money off of your idea. You will definitely need an adult to help you apply for a patent. It can be a complicated and expensive process. But if you think that people will want to buy your invention, it is well worth it.

WORDS TO KNOW

disk harrow—A farming tool that creates many even rows of earth for planting crops.

electric—Using energy made from moving electrons, usually through wires.

electron—A tiny electrical part of every material thing in the world.

electronic—Using electrons

generator—A machine that changes power from a source like gasoline into electricity.

investor—Someone who supplies money for an idea and expects to earn more money in return.

laboratory—A workshop for scientific experiments and tests.

mechanical—Using moving parts.

weld—To press and melt two pieces of metal together by running electricity through them.

working model—An early example of an invention that works. It may be very small or without all the details of the final piece.

LEARN MORE

Books

Richter, Joanne. *Inventing The Television*. New York;
St. Catharines, Ont.: Crabtree Pub., 2006.

Roberts, Russell. *Philo Farnsworth Invents TV*. Hockessin,
Del.: Mitchell Lane Publishers, 2005.

Woods, Michael and Mary B. *The History of Communication*.
Minneapolis, Minn.: Lerner Publications, 2005.

Internet Addresses

To learn more about Philo T. Farnsworth, visit these websites:
Fact Monster: People: Philo T. Farnsworth, Inventor
<http://www.factmonster.com/biography/var/philotfarnsworth.html>
The Great Idea Finder: Inventor Philo T. Farnsworth
<www.ideafinder.com/history/inventors/farnsworth.htm>

If you want to learn more about becoming an inventor, check
out these websites:
Inventnow.org
http://www.inventnow.org/
The Inventive Kids Blog
http://www.inventivekids.com/
The U.S. Patent and Trademark Office Kid's Pages
http://www.uspto.gov/web/offices/ac/ahrpa/opa/kids/index.html

INDEX